MUSCLE CAR GREATS

By Peter C. Sessler

Designed by Matthew Blitz

Contents

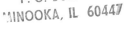
This edition published in 1992 by SMITHMARK Publishers Inc., 112 Madison Avenue, New York, NY 10016

SMITHMARK Books are available for bulk purchase for sales promotion and premium use. For details, write or telephone the Manager of Special Sales, SMITHMARK Publishers Inc., 112 Madison Avenue, New York, NY 10016   (212) 532-6600.

ISBN 0-8317-6191-1

Printed in Hong Kong

INTRODUCTION

Few eras in automotive history can equal the muscle-car era in terms of excitement. It was a time when Detroit manufacturers kept bringing out new models and new engines, not only in an attempt to outdo each other, but also to grab a larger share of the growing, emerging youth market. And what did the youth market want? It wanted cars that looked great, went fast and also conveyed a sense of power. Detroit obliged willingly—by 1968, 10 percent of the U.S. market was taken by musclecars. At the time, though, these performance cars were not known as musclecars, but rather, Supercars.

The roots of the musclecar era lie in the 1950s. Detroit did build powerful, distinctive cars, but most of them were full-size models. It was difficult for the young buyer to acquire such a car, but also, the full-size models just didn't have a youthful image.

Looking back, it seems that Pontiac's action in 1964 to install large passenger car V8 engines in its intermediate models was a brilliant marketing move. Take a regular 2-door interme-diate, install a larger engine, a nice set of wheels and tires, a louder exhaust system, give it a fancy-sounding name and some distinctive identification and there you have it—the GTO was born. The GTO was distinctive and, just as important from Pontiac's point of view, it was cheap to produce. Still, the GTO's success was due more to good timing than anything else. Pontiac never expected it to sell as well as it did; it happened to be the right car at the right time, just as the Mustang was.

Within a few year, General Motors' other divisions (with the exception of Cadillac) brought out their own musclecars; name-plates such as the Chevelle SS, the Buick Gran Sport and the Oldsmobile 4-4-2 soon gained a following. Ford wasn't as suc-cessful with the Fairlane GT and later the Torino, but Chrysler came on like gangbusters with its intermediate musclecars such as the Plymouth Road Runner and Dodge Charger.

Following typical Detroit thinking, if musclecars are selling so well, why not apply the same formula to other models? Soon there were muscle ponycars, muscle compacts and muscle full-size cars.

But it couldn't last. By 1971, it was all over. There were too many different models chasing too few buyers. Musclecars were no longer inexpensive and, coupled with increasingly higher insurance premiums, it was becoming too difficult for the young buyer to buy a full-fledged musclecar. And many just wanted a musclecar image without the bother of maintaining a guzzler.

Detroit complied—big engines were dropped because they weren't selling anymore, but also, it was becoming more difficult and expensive for Detroit to meet increasingly stringent emission standards. If a large market segment still wanted high-horse-power engines, there is no doubt that Detroit would have found a way.

During the 1980s, musclecars were rediscovered. Unlike previous "old" cars, cars of the Sixties could still be driven regularly—in fact, it is only through driving that musclecars can be fully appreciated. Yes, these cars are big, impractical and uneconomical—and some even consider them socially irresponsible. But they are unique and they also have a quality that is lacking in many of today's cars—they're fun!

The cars shown in the following pages are taken from the files of CSK Publishing Co., Inc., publishers of MuscleCars, Vette, High Performance Mopar, Muscle Mustangs & Fast Fords and High Performance Pontiac magazines. These beautiful cars are "correct"—that is, they are original and unmodified and they look the same as they did back in their heyday, with the only possible exception being tires.

So go ahead, and enjoy. Cars like this will never be made again.

INTERMEDIATE MUSCLE

1964-65

By all accounts, Pontiac has been credited with building the first true musclecar, the GTO, in 1964. Prior to its introduction, the big-horsepower cars were full-size models, such as the 409-powered Chevrolet Impala or the 427-cubic-inch Ford Galaxies. There was also the Corvette, which offered plenty of performance, but whose high price and two-seat configuration tended to limit its appeal.

What Pontiac did was to put its largest, most powerful V8 engine—in this case a 389 with a four-barrel carburetor rated at 325 hp—in the midsize Tempest body. Naturally, in keeping with a performance image, a three-speed manual transmission with a floor shifter was standard as was a heavy-duty suspension. And, of course, the GTO had dual exhausts and premium tires. The result was a high-performance car that had considerably more youth appeal than the full-size performance cars, which to many, looked like "Dad's" car.

As important to the GTO's image was the GTO name itself. The term GTO stood for Gran Turismo Omologato, which described a class of cars that raced on international road-race circuits. The car that originated the use of the GTO name as a separate model

The 1964 GTO heralded a new dawn— The Musclecar Era—with a mid-size body and a 325-horse 389 under the hood.

was Ferrari. The Ferrari GTO was a high-priced, hand-built exotic, while the Tempest GTO obviously was not.

Following typical Detroit fashion, the GTO was available with a long list of options, including a four-speed manual transmission and a higher-horsepower version of the 389-cubic-inch engine rated at 348 hp, which sported

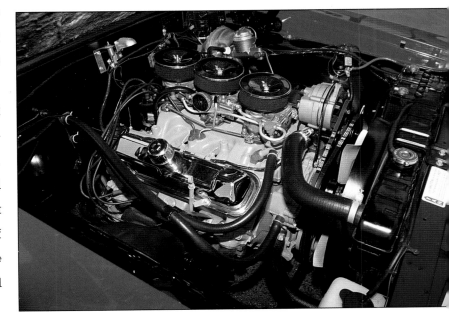

a 3x2bbl. intake setup. The GTO was also built as a convertible.

The result? Fourteen-second quarter-mile times, in an extremely appealing package and at an affordable price.

Pontiac had intended a run of 5,000 GTOs for 1964, but when the model year ended, a total 32,450 were produced. Clearly, the GTO was a lot more popular than Pontiac executives expected.

The 1965 GTO, which showed styling changes—most notably the use of vertical headlights—proved to be even more popular, with 75,352 sold.

Chevy shoehorned its new-for-'65 big-block "Rat motor" into its Chevelle platform. Remarkably, only 201 '65s were ever built.

1966 Pontiac GTO.

1965 Oldsmobile F-85 Cutlass 4-4-2.

In the meantime, it was obvious that the competition was taken by surprise. At Chevrolet, the midsize intermediate was the Chevelle and it was available with the Super Sport option, but with only a 327-cubic-inch engine, it was no match for the GTO. The first true muscle Super Sport Chevelle became available in late 1965, the so-called Z16 optioned Chevelle, which packed a 375-hp 396-cubic-inch big-block engine. However, its impact was minimal, as only 201 were built. Still, it foreshadowed what was to come from Chevrolet.

Oldsmobile scrambled to get out its version of the GTO. This was the F85 Cutlass 4-4-2, and it was powered by a 330-cubic-inch Oldsmobile engine. In 1965, engine size was increased to 400 cubic inches. The name 4-4-2 stood for four-speed transmission, four-barrel carburetor and dual exhausts. The Cutlass 4-4-2 proved to be a very quick street performer, but like the Super Sport Chevelle, sales were very low.

On the other hand, it took staid Buick until 1965 to introduce the Skylark Gran Sport and it proved to be more popular than the Oldsmobile 4-4-2 with 15,780 sold. Again, as with other GM intermediates, the Buick followed the formula set by Pontiac, stuffing a large V8 into the intermediate body.

Meanwhile, Ford was busy with the spectacular success of the Mustang and

1965 Buick Gran Sport.

1967 Chevelle SS396.

didn't do much in the way of promoting its intermediate, the Fairlane, as a musclecar, mainly because there wasn't enough room in the 1964-65 Fairlane engine compartment for a big-block engine. The stoutest V8 that could fit was the same 271-hp 289-cubic-inch V8 that could also be found in the lighter Mustang.

At Chrysler, Dodge and Plymouth midsize offerings could not compete in terms of styling, though Chrysler engines were strong. Cautious Chrysler Corporation was still trying to recover from the styling excesses of the early 1960s and would not introduce a midsize performance musclecar with its own distinct identity until 1967.

1966-67

During the '60s, General Motors was on a two-year body/styling cycle. This meant that every two years, the body would be restyled; for example, 1966-67 GTOs shared the same basic body shell, with minor trim variations differentiating the two years. The midsize platform, known within GM as the A-body, was changed again for 1968 and restyled again for 1970-72. Beneath the skin, though, all General Motors intermediates shared the same basic suspensions, rear axles and transmissions, differing in suspension tuning and engines, as each Division had

1967 Oldsmobile 4-4-2.

The 1966 Buick GS's styling was evolutionary.

A very rare 1966 427 Fairlane, which featured 2 4-bbl. carburetors.

its own engines. By corporate edict, engine size was limited to 400 cubic inches on all intermediates.

The GTO was restyled in 1966. It looked very similar to the 1965s, but the car had a more rounded, Coke-bottle look. Engine availability was the same—versions of the 389-cubic-inch V8 with the four-barrel carburetor of the 360-hp Tri-Power setup. The GTO was the undisputed musclecar leader with a total 96,496 sold—the highest GTO sales would ever reach.

Important mechanical changes were made to the GTO in 1967. First, the 389 engine was bored out to displace 400 cubic inches and the exotic Tri-Power carburetion system was replaced by a more mundane single four-barrel. Still, the engine was rated at a powerful 360 hp. In addition, 1967 was the first year for the Ram Air induction option, which routed cool air to the carburetor. As with other GM intermediates, the superior three-speed Turbohydramatic automatic trasmission became available. Still the king, the GTO's sales fell a bit to 81,722 units.

In 1966, Chevrolet finally got it together and introduced a brace of 396-cubic-inch engines for the Super Sport Chevelle, in three horsepower levels. The standard engine put out 325 hp, while optional engines were rated at 360 and 375 hp. Styling on

1967 Plymouth
Belvedere GTX.

the Chevelle was a bit more conservative (read: plainer) than the GTO; all that distinguished it from the regular Chevelle models were two simulated hood air intakes, an SS grille, rear taillight panel emblems and Super Sport script on the rear fenders along with special lower panel moldings. It was an easy, fairly inexpensive way for the factory to spruce up the car. Sales were impressive, at 72,272 units.

The 1967 Super Sport got the usual facelift. A mildly restyled nose and tail and new wraparound taillights were the most noticeable changes. In the engine department, the middle 396-cubic-incher was downrated 10 hp to 350 hp while the famous Turbohydramatic automatic transmission became available. Other mechanical improvements shared by all 1967 GM intermediates included the availability of front disc brakes.

Sharing the same A-body platform with its tunnelled rear window was the Oldsmobile Cutlass 4-4-2. Like the GTO and Chevelle, the 4-4-2 got its special identification in keeping with a performance image. Interestingly, the 400-cubic-inch engine could be had with triple two-barrel carburetion, raising power to 360 hp. This engine, however, was available only for 1966. The 1967 4-4-2s were very similar to the '66s, with the most noticeable change being the addition of special hood louvers.

Over at Buick, the Skylark Gran Sport, although a strong-performing car, didn't have quite the same impact as the GTO or

1968 Buick GS 400.

Chevelle and this was reflected in its sales figures: 13,816 in 1966 and 17,405 for 1967. It seemed to be just a matter of having a performance car to offer, hoping that the buyer would eventually trade up to a more traditional Buick. All Gran Sports were powered by the Buick 400-cubic-inch engine, but a smaller 340-cubic-inch engine was introduced for 1967 for the GS340. It did not prove popular.

Ford's Fairlane was restyled for 1966, and had to play catch-up with other muscle intermediates. The top Fairlane model was the Fairlane GT, which could be powered by an optional 390-cubic-inch V8 rated at 315 hp. Even so, the 390 wasn't much of a performer. However, to get recognition and to qualify the Fairlane for drag racing, about 70 were built with the 427-cubic-inch engine—a real powerhouse, to be sure. Most of these cars came with two four-barrel carburetion for 425 hp.

At Ford's other Division, the Mercury Cyclone GT parallelled the Fairlane as they both shared the same body platform and drivetrain.

Chrysler's intermediates were restyled in 1965, but it wasn't until 1966 that the musclecar's era most powerful engine made its debut—the Chrysler 426 Hemi. The Hemi, as it has been referred to, was a street version of Chrysler's most powerful race engine. Differing from other musclecar engines, the Hemi came with hemispherical combustion chambers (hence the name). This design enabled the engine to "breathe" and keep on producing power at the higher rpm ranges when other engines would be wheezing. This meant that Hemi-equipped cars would not only have tremendous acceleration from a standing start but also would keep on accelerating just as hard, if not harder, at higher engine speeds. Only a handful of cars could keep up with a Hemi.

Chrysler began installing the 426 Hemi in 1966 Plymouth Belvederes and Satellites, and in Dodge Coronets and Chargers. It was an expensive engine option with fewer than 2,500 Chrysler intermediates getting the Hemi.

Chrysler's muscle intermediates didn't begin to have much of an impact until the 1967 model year. It was then that Chrysler followed the same procedure established at General Motors—take your basic intermediate body platform and install a large engine while giving the cars a separate, appealing identity. Just as important, Chrysler began to market these cars far more

The 1968 Plymouth Road Runner—an instant hit.

1968 Plymouth Belvedere GTX.

aggressively. At Plymouth, there was the Belvedere GTX, while over at Dodge, there was the Coronet R/T. Except for styling, both of these cars were the same under the skin. The standard engine on both was the new 440-cubic-inch V8 rated at 375 hp with only one engine option available, the 425-hp 426 Hemi.

Although Plymouth and Dodge were late in bringing on their muscle intermediates, they quickly earned a reputation as the musclecars to beat. They may have lacked the pizzaz of GM's musclecars, but they made an impact as a no-compromise street racer.

1968-69

While individual model sales were declining, model proliferation was expanding. Ford brought new engines and a restyled intermediate, the Torino, while Chrysler, as we shall see, was busier than ever. As competition between the manufacturers grew fiercer, the graphics and colors used became wilder and wilder.

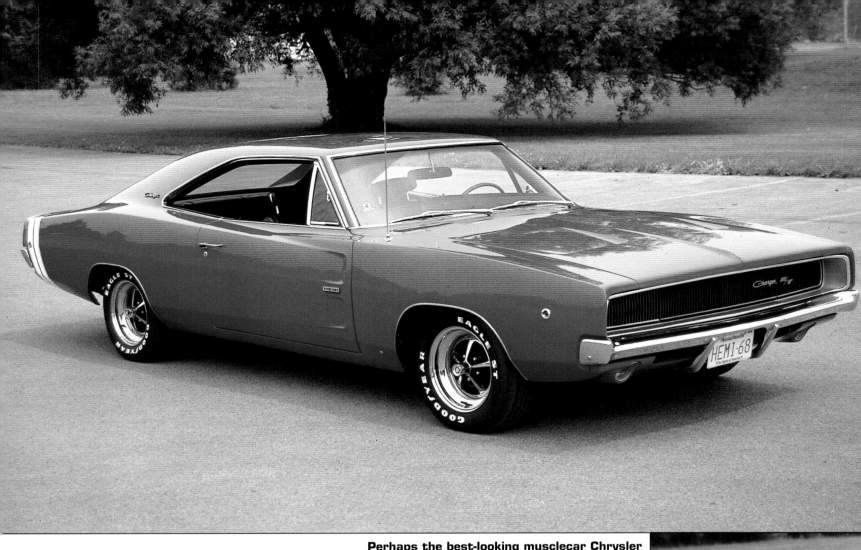

Perhaps the best-looking musclecar Chrysler ever built was the 1968 Dodge Charger.

All the GM intermediates were restyled for 1968. The GTO's standard engine was still a 400-incher, now putting out 350 hp, but the GTO's new styling was outstanding. Curvier than the 1966-67 cars, the GTO stood out from the rest with its unique Endura front bumper, which was painted to match the car's body color while the grille housed hidden headlights. Top engine option was the Ram Air III rated at 366 hp.

The 1969 GTOs got the usual styling refinements, but more exciting was the introduction of the GTO Judge, available as a coupe and a convertible. Differing from regular GTOs, the Judge got tri-colored front and rear fender stripes, "The Judge" decals and a large 60-inch rear deck spoiler. Standard engine was the 366-hp Ram Air III with the more powerful 370-hp Ram Air IV optional. The Judge was originally conceived as a low-budget musclecar, like Plymouth's Road Runner.

**The 1969 Chevelle SS396 overtook
Pontiac's GTO as the premier musclecar.**

**The awesome 1969¹/2
6-bbl. Plymouth Road Runner.**

Chevrolet continued to offer the Chevelle SS396. Engine availability didn't change; there were still three versions of the 396-cubic-inch big-block. There were a couple of reasons that 1969 turned out to be significant for the Chevelle. First, it outsold the GTO, 86,307 to 72,287. Secondly, only a very small number of cars, 400, were built with the L89 engine option. This was the same engine as the regular L78 375-hp engine except that it had aluminum cylinder heads. There were also 323 cars built with the 425-hp, 427-cubic-inch engine under the COPO (Central Office Processing Order) program.

The Oldsmobile 4-4-2 became a separate model line in 1968, rather than an option package on the Cutlass. Standard engine remained at 400 cubic inches rated at 350 hp with the hot W-30 package optional on '69s, which offered air induction and 360

1969 Ford Torino with 428 Cobra Jet power.

hp. The 1968 4-4-2s got a blacked-out grille with a central 442 emblem, while 1969s got a split grille arrangement. The optional air induction system placed the air intakes just beneath the front bumper.

There was also a variant of the 4-4-2, the Hurst/Olds. These special cars were modified by George Hurst's (of Hurst shifter fame) Hurst Corporation, and came with a 390-hp, 455-cubic-inch Olds V8, special paint (Silver for 1968, white/gold for 1969) and a list of unique options.

Buick's Gran Sport continued to be offered during 1968-69. Perhaps the most conservatively styled of all GM intermediates of that period, the Gran Sport can be identified by its sharp bodyside crease beginning at the front fender and ending just in front of the rear wheel opening. The Buick Gran Sport was available as the GS350 with a 350-cubic-inch engine, or as the GS400 with the more

1969 Oldsmobile 4-4-2.

The **1969 Dodge Super Bee** was similar in concept to the Road Runner, but wasn't as popular.

potent 400-cubic-inch engine. Convertibles were available only as a GS400. Styling for the 1969s was very similar except that an eggshell-type grille was used.

Over at Ford, the Fairlane was restyled for 1968. An upgraded version, the Torino, also made its debut in '68, but in 1969 the Torino became a separate model. The 427 engine, rated at 390 hp and available only with an automatic transmission, was the top engine option. Few were sold, and in the spring, the 428 Cobra Jet became the top engine. In 1969, the Torino Cobra took the top performance spot.

There was also the Talladega, essentially a modified Torino designed for use on the NASCAR stock car tracks. It featured an extended nose for better aerodynamics and all were powered by the 428 Cobra Jet engine. Only 745 were built.

Complementing the Talladega was the Mercury Cyclone Spoiler II, which got a similar extended nose treatment.

Plymouth continued offering the GTX, but the most important addition to Plymouth's musclecar offerings was the 1968 midyear introduction of the Road Runner. The Road Runner was an entry-level musclecar, bereft of most conveniences but offering plenty of performance. The standard engine displaced 383 cubic inches with the 426 Hemi being optional. Capitalizing on the Road Runner cartoon character, the car was an instant hit. Following the usual styl-

A rare Dodge Charger derivative is the 1969 Daytona, designed for the NASCAR super speedways.

ing changes for 1969, Plymouth again released another performance powerhouse, the Road Runner 6-bbl. This Road Runner came with a special version of the 440-cubic-inch engine, pumping out 390 hp with the help of 3x2bbl carburetion. The idea was to offer the same performance (or close to it) as the 426 Hemi engine, but at a lower price. Like most other Road Runners, the 6-bbl was a pretty spartan car. Another addition to the Road Runner line in 1969 was a Road Runner convertible.

Dodge was just as busy in 1968-69. The Coronet R/T was still available, appealing to buyers who liked comfort as well as performance. When the Road Runner came out, Dodge responded with the Super Bee and again, the Super Bee 6-Pack later in 1969. Most significant was the redesigned Dodge Charger, debuting in 1968. This was the best-looking car to come out of Chrysler styling studios in the 1960s, and was, arguably, the quintessential musclecar. The performance Charger model was the Charger R/T, which mirrored the Coronet R/T in terms of engine availability—the 375-hp, 440-cubic-inch engine standard, and the 426 Hemi optional.

In 1969, the Charger was restyled slightly, but there were also two Charger variants. The first was the Charger 500, which

The infamous 1970 Chevelle SS454.

featured a flush grille and a redesigned rear window. These aerodynamic improvements were intended to make the Charger more competitive on the NASCAR race circuit. The Charger 500 was an improvement, but Ford's Talladega was better, which forced Dodge to come out with something considerably more radical, the Charger Daytona. The Daytona had a special nose cone extension and a very tall rear wing spoiler. It really stood out. Production of these two models was low—500 Charger 500s and 503 Daytonas.

1970-71

The year 1970 is considered a high point of the musclecar era because great styling and the largest, most powerful engines made their debut, especially at General Motors, which finally lifted its ban on engines larger than 400 cubic inches on intermediates. At Buick, Oldsmobile and Pontiac, the largest engines now measured 455 cubic inches; Chevrolet's big-block displaced 454 cubic inches.

Unlike the extensive model change that occurred in 1968, the 1970-71 GM intermediates were basically cleaned-up, restyled versions of 1969 models. In fact, breaking with the past, the basic 1968 body platforms would continue until 1972.

1970 Pontiac GTO Judge.

1970 Dodge Coronet R/T with its odd loop bumpers. This one is powered by a 440 6-Pack.

The Pontiac GTO and Judge continued with 400- and 455-cubic-inch engines, but 1970 turned out to be the last year for the Ram Air III and IV engines. The new 455 turned out to be a great street engine with its 500 ft.-lbs. of torque. Most noticeable was the new, aggressive front end treatment, which was shared by the Judge as well.

In 1971, GTOs got the usual restyling with a redesigned front end. Although all GM engines were slightly detuned for 1971, the GTO was still a very strong performer, but 1971 turned out to be the last year for the Judge due to sluggish sales. The GTO continued on in 1972-73, but as an option package on the LeMans and not as a separate model line. In 1974, its last year, the GTO became an option on the Ventura compact, a sad ending for a once-proud marque.

The Super Sport Chevelle reached its height in 1970. In addition to the SS396, there was now the SS454 Chevelle with the new 454-cubic-inch big-block. Two versions were available: the LS6, which put out 450 hp, and a milder LS5, rated at 360 hp. The LS6-powered Chevelles have an awesome performance image. Besides the new engines, the 1970 Chevelle got a new four-headlight grille.

The 1971 Super Sport Chevelle continued on without the LS6 version of the 454. Headlight configuration was changed to a single light per side. Nineteen seventy-one is considered to be the

1970 Oldsmobile 4-4-2.

last year of the true high-performance Super Sport Chevelle because the engines still put out lots of horsepower. Even though the 396 and 454 engines were available in 1972, they were considerably less powerful, due to Chevrolet's inability to produce a high-horsepower engine that

1970 Oldsmobile 4-4-2 Indy Pace Car.

would meet the current emission regulations. Even so, musclecars weren't selling well anymore, so it is unlikely that high-horsepower engines would have sold any more cars.

The 4-4-2's engine got bumped up to 455 cubic inches in 1970-71. The hot setup was still the W-30 engine option, which included the 370-hp 455 V8 and a new fiberglass hood with functional hood scoops. Styling, though similar to the 1968-69s, was a bit more aggressive.

The 1970-71 Buick Gran Sports also exhibited better styling, eliminating the cumbersome side creases of the 1968-69 Gran

Sports. The big Buick 455-cubic-inch engine, under Stage 1 guise, was a tremendous performer. Like other GM intermediates, the Buick Gran Sports were laid to rest after the 1972 model year.

At Ford, the Torino was restyled for 1970. The car was larger, but the styling was a bit curvier and more fluid. A new 429 Cobra Jet engine replaced the aging 428. The big Ford, though, never enjoyed the popularity of GM or Chrysler intermediates. The big 429 was

A high point for Buick was the 1970 GSX, whose unusual interior and exterior treatment made it stand out.

carried over into 1971 with increasingly declining sales. Musclecar performance was finally laid to rest when the restyled 1972 models emphasized traditional American car values—big-car ride and luxury.

Musclecars continued their prominence at Chrysler through the 1971 model year. At Plymouth, the Road Runner and GTX got a facelift, but the cars themselves still resembled the 1968-69 models. All the big engines were still available: the 375-hp 440, the 390-hp 440 6-bbl and, of course, the 426 Hemi. Plymouth brought out the Road Runner Superbird, which resembled the 1969 Charger Daytona

The ultimate Road Runner—the 1970 Superbird.

A rare 1970 Plymouth
Road Runner convertible
with 440 6-bbl. power.

1971 was the last year for
the brutish, high-powered
Road Runner—though the
name would continue.

with its extended nose and high rear wing.

The Dodge Coronet R/T was changed, this time featuring an odd dual-loop front bumper design. The beautiful Charger still used the same bodyshell, but for 1970 it, too, got a loop front bumper. Both Plymouth and Dodge intermediates were restyled for 1971 for a totally new look. The GTX and Road Runner shared the same body and the engines were carried over from 1970. The Coronet R/T was dropped for 1971, while the Super Bee became a Charger-based derivative.

The 1971 Ford Torino with the massive 429CJ. Shaker scoop was standard with the 429CJ.

The Dodge and Plymouth intermediates were still in production until 1974, using the same body shells. Engines from 1972, however, were considerably less muscular as the top Chrysler performance engines, the 426 Hemi and 440 6-bbl, were dropped.

Thus, for all practical purposes, 1971 marked the end of the muscle era. Cars would still be produced that echoed the performance image of the musclecars, but that's as far as they went. It would take about 15 years before Detroit began producing performance cars again, but even so, these new performance cars just aren't the same. The old musclecars were crude, crass and blatant, but that's what made them unique.

The 1971 Charger was totally restyled—yet was still available with the 440 6-pack motor.

A pair of 1966 Shelby GT350H Mustangs, which, believe it or not, were rental cars. The "H" stood for "Hertz."

PONY MUSCLE

What car typifies the 1960s more than any other? The answer is probably the Ford Mustang, which was introduced in April 1964. Its smaller size, long hood/short deck, availability of three different body styles, a long option list and low cost made the Mustang a popular car with young and old alike. Ford tried to make the Mustang a car for all. For example, it could be optioned out as a thrifty daily driver or as a high-performance car and anything in between.

The hot Mustangs were those that got the GT option package, which was available with a 225-hp 289-cubic-inch V8 or a high-performance 271-hp version of the same engine. Mustangs equipped with the 271-hp engine became known as K-cars, because the letter "K" was used in the vehicle identification number (VIN) to identify the high-horsepower engine. The 271-hp engine made the Mustang quicker, but it wasn't in the same league as musclecars such as the GTO.

The 1967 Shelby GT500 Mustang got big-block power— a 360-hp 428.

The 1967 Camaro
SS396 with the L78
375-hp engine option.

It didn't really matter, as Ford was selling all the Mustangs that could be produced. For those who wanted a truly high-performance Mustang, there was the Shelby Mustang GT350. The Shelby Mustangs were modified by Carroll Shelby to his specifications and featured a slew of no-nonsense standard performance features that enabled the Mustang to perform with the best. The 1965-66 Shelby Mustangs came with distinctive hood/roof/rear deck stripes. In an unusual move, in 1966, Hertz, the rental company, purchased 1000 Shelby Mustangs for use as rental cars. Most were painted black with gold stripes, but there were a few red, green, blue and white cars built as well.

It took General Motors two years to come out with cars that could compete with the Mustang, the Chevrolet Camaro and the Pontiac Firebird. These were similar in concept to the Mustang and were intended to appeal to the same buyers. Chrysler had the Barracuda since 1964, but it was never a serious contender.

The Mustang was scheduled to be redesigned for the 1967 model year. Ford, though, found out that when the Camaro would finally be introduced it could be ordered with an optional 396-cubic-inch big-block V8 and the Firebird could also be had with the 400-cubic-inch Pontiac V8. Even the Barracuda could be ordered with a 383-cubic-inch V8.

This prompted Ford to make available as an option the 390-cubic-inch V8 that powered Thunderbirds, Fairlanes and Galaxies. A horsepower war was on.

The 1967 Mustangs could be powered with the 390 engine along with the GT option package. It was a good performer, considerably quicker than the previous 271-hp 289-powered Mustangs of 1965-66. Unfortunately, it was no match for SS396-powered Camaros or Firebirds with the 400 engine.

Similar to the Camaro,
Pontiac's Firebird got a
different front grille and
taillight treatment, not to
mention Pontiac power.

There was one Mustang that was as quick, if not quicker. When the regular Mustangs were modified to accept the larger 390 engine, the Shelby Mustangs, still based on the regular Mustang, could also be built with the 390 engine. However, rather than using the 390 engine, Shelby elected to use the 428-cubic-inch Police Interceptor engine, which had the exact same physical specs as the 390. To give it extra punch, the engine was outfitted with a 2x4bbl. intake manifold set up for 360 hp. Besides that big engine, the Shelby looked a lot tougher than regular Mustangs with its scoops and stripes. The 289-cubic-inch engined Shelby Mustang GT350 was still available, while those powered by the 428 were named GT500.

The hot Camaro was the Super Sport Camaro. Engine availability was the 350-cubic-inch small-block with 300 hp and two versions of the 396-cubic-inch V8 putting out 325 or 375 hp. Super Sport Camaros came with a distinctive front wraparound stripe and complementing SS emblems on the grille and taillight panel.

Little was said about another Camaro that came out in 1967—the Z/28. The Z/28 came with a 302-cubic-inch version of Chevrolet's small-block V8, which was rated at 290 hp. The emphasis on the Z/28 was achieving a balance between handling, braking and acceleration, whereas the typical musclecar put more emphasis on acceleration. In addition, such a car was needed in order to homologate the Camaro for the Sports Car Club of America's (SCCA) new Trans Am road race series. Only 602 were sold.

You could identify the Z/28 by its wide hood and deck stripes and Rally wheels. It was only in late 1968 that the car's Z/28 emblems appeared.

The 1967 Camaro was chosen to be the Pace car for the Indianapolis 500. In addition to the four cars used for the race, there were 100 Pace cars built for use by various race officials and dignitaries.

Sharing the same body as the Camaro, the Pontiac Firebird got a different nose and rear end treatment. Two versions of the Pontiac 400 V8 were available, both rated at 325 hp, although the more powerful 400 Ram Air engine was the same one that powered the GTO with 360 hp.

In 1967, Mercury also brought out its Pony car, the Cougar. Sharing the same drivetrain as the Mustang, it was heavier but more luxurious and could be equipped with a leather interior.

1968

The 1968¹/2 Cobra Jet Mustang. This is a rare pre-production model.

In 1968, Ford added another engine to the Mustang's option list, a 390-hp 427. This was a derivative of Ford's successful, all-out race engine and, as it looked the same outwardly as the 390, there was no problem fitting it into the Mustang's engine compartment. However, the real problem with the engine was cost. It was an expensive engine option, and Ford withdrew it only three months into the model year, letting the outclassed 390 carry on as the Mustang's top engine option. This was not to last, however, as in April of 1968, the 428 Cobra Jet engine became available on the Mustang. This engine was a conglomeration of 427 and 428 parts and the result was a very muscular street engine, which could be produced and sold at a reasonable cost. The 428CJ was rated at a conservative 335 hp.

The Shelby Mustangs were restyled and when the 428CJ engine came out, Shelby Mustangs with this engine were identified as the GT500KR. Reportedly, the KR stood for King of the Road. Another model joined the Shelby lineup—a convertible that had a unique, vinyl-covered roll bar.

The 428 Cobra Jet engine made the Mustang a street terror.

The Camaro and Firebird continued in 1968 with few changes. The top engine on the Firebird was the Ram Air II with 340 hp.

During this time, the Camaro became a favorite with certain performance-oriented dealers, as a basis for an even more muscular Camaro. The best known of these dealer-modified Camaros were the Yenko Camaros, which sported 427-cubic-inch engines.

1968 Shelby GT350—as mean-looking as they come.

The 1968 Javelin was American Motors'
entry into the ponycar market.

In 1968, American Motors, the smallest of the Detroit auto manufacturers, brought out a ponycar—the Javelin. It was a good-looking car, and it could be had with a 390-cubic-inch V8. Later in the model year, American Motors brought out the two-seater AMX, basically a shortened Javelin. Both cars shared the same drivetrain.

1969

The Mustang had a big year in 1969, being restyled with a more aggressive frontal appearance and a sleeker fastback body style. In addition to the GT, a new performance model, the Mach 1, was introduced. The Mach 1 got the race car treatment look, with a blacked-out hood and a hood scoop, hood pins, sport mirrors and reflective side stripes. Several engines were available with the Mach 1: a 351, the old 390 and the 428 Cobra Jet, which could be had with an unusual "Shaker" hood scoop. Later in the model year, the Boss 429 Mustang was released. It was powered by a 429-cubic-inch engine with modified hemi-type

The 1969 Mustang Mach 1 makes a very strong statement, even when standing still.

The understated 1969 Boss 429 Mustang.

The 1969 Boss 302 was a Mustang that
could handle as well as accelerate.

aluminum cylinder heads. Unlike other Mustangs, the Boss 429 had a very understated appearance with just minimal identification and no stripes or graphics. The big 429 was installed in Mustangs, enabling Ford to use the engine on the NASCAR stock car circuit.

Another special Mustang, designed to compete with the Camaro Z/28, was the Boss 302. This Mustang, unlike the Boss 429, had lots of blacked-out body panels, a front spoiler, stripes and optional rear wings and rear window slats. It was powered by a special version of the 302 engine and put out 290 hp, the same as the Chevrolet Z/28.

Only 852 Mustangs got the Boss 429 engine, while there were 1,628 Boss 302s built.

The Shelby Mustangs were also restyled—this time looking quite different from regular production Mustangs. Two models were available: the GT350, with a 351-cubic-inch engine, and the GT500, powered by the 428 Cobra Jet. As in 1968, there were two bodystyles available—the sportsroof and the convertible. The complete model run wasn't sold in 1969; the few hundred leftovers were resold as 1970 models. These cars got two hood stripes and a Boss 302 spoiler to distinguish them from the 1969 models.

Unlike the Boss 429, the Boss 302's graphics stood out.

1969 Shelby GT500 featured totally different styling from the '68's.

The Camaro and Firebird were facelifted for 1969. The Super Sport Camaro remained the premier Camaro performance model with the 396-cubic-inch engine, but the Z/28's popularity, by this time, had really caught on, with 20,302 sold.

There were also 69 Camaros built with the 427 ZL1 aluminum block engine under the COPO (Central Office Production Order) program. In addition, at least 201 Camaros got the iron-block version of this engine, with most of these being sold through Don Yenko's Chevrolet dealership.

As in 1967, the 1969 Camaro was chosen to be the pace car for the Indianapolis 500 race. To commemorate this event, 3,675 Pace Car replicas were built for sale to the public. They were all Super Sport convertibles finished in Dover White paint with a unique orange houndstooth interior.

The Pontiac Firebird got a stronger version of the Pontiac 400-cubic-inch V8, the Ram Air IV rated at 345 hp. More important was the little-noticed addition of a new model, the Firebird Trans Am, as only 697 were built, eight being convertibles. The Trans Am would become the premier performance Firebird model, and is still with us today.

American Motors' Javelin and AMX got a slight trim change, but in other respects were unchanged.

Mercury's Cougar got a new model in '69, the Eliminator, which could be powered by Ford's 428CJ engine, again appealing to those who wanted muscle with a bit more class.

At Plymouth, even though the Barracuda could be had with

The first Firebird Trans Am was a 1969 model.

1969 SS Camaro Pace Car Edition.

1969 "Yenko"
Camaros.

1969 SS396 Camaro with RS package that featured hidden headlamps.

383 and even 440-cubic-inch engines, the car just didn't catch on, being outsold even by American Motors' Javelin. The car still used the same basic styling as the 1967 models. Plymouth fans had to wait another year before a totally restyled Barracuda was introduced.

1970 Mustang Mach 1 with the optional 428CJ Ram Air engine.

1969 Z/28 Camaro—lean, taut, and fast, especially when equipped with a rare pair of 4-bbl. carbs.

In 1970, the Firebird line received a major updating. Model choices expanded to include this Formula 400.

1970

Pony musclecars reached a high point in 1970, with new engines, new models and two serious newcomers from Chrysler— the Plymouth Barracuda and the Dodge Challenger.

The Mustang, still the leader in terms of sales, used the same body but did get a different front-end treatment, reverting to the single headlight theme. The Mach 1 got a new 351-cubic-inch engine, the 351 Cleveland; the 390 was dropped and the 428CJ was still the top engine option. The Mustang GT was no longer available.

The Boss 429 was carried over, distinguished by its black hood scoop for 1970. Only 499 were built. The Boss 302 proved to be more popular, as 7,013 were sold, benefiting from new stripes and graphics and a new series of Graber paint colors.

The Cougar Eliminator's engine availability increased to three— the 290-hp Boss 302, the 300-hp 351 Cleveland or the 335-hp 428 CJ. Stripes, scoops, spoilers and enhanced paint colors made the Eliminator stand out.

The newly restyled Camaro for 1970. This is a rare SS396.

The 1970 Boss 302 Mustang proved to be the most popular, with 7,013 produced.

The Camaro and Firebird were totally restyled for 1970, bearing no resemblance to their predecessors. Still, the performance Camaro models were the same—the Super Sport and Z/28. Top engine on the SS396 was still rated at 375 hp its last year, while the Z/28 came with a 350-cubic-inch version on the small-block rated at 360 hp.

At Pontiac, the model lineup was juggled some-what, with the performance models being the Formula and the Trans Am. The Formula received two forward-mounted hood scoops, while the Trans Am got a reverse-mounted "Shaker"-type of scoop. The biggest en-gine on both of these models was the 400-cubic-inch Ram Air IV.

The Javelin and AMX got new grille treatments for 1970, as American Motors lacked the resources for a major restyle. Top dog engine remained the 390-cubic-inch V8.

Better late than never describes Chrysler's 1970 ponycars— the Plymouth Barracuda and Dodge Challenger. Both were based on the Chrysler intermediate body platforms and, as such, could accommodate all the Chrysler big-block engines.

The premier Barracuda performance model was the 'Cuda, available as a hardtop or convertible. The 'Cuda could be had with a variety of engines: the 340 small-block, the 383, 440, 440-6bbl. and the 426 Hemi. Wild colors, spoilers, wings, scoops, big tires and graphics characterized the 'Cuda.

There was also the AAR 'Cuda. This model was designed to compete with the Boss 302 and Z/28 Camaro. It was powered by a 3x2bbl. version of the 340-cubic-inch small-block V8 and it featured a side exit exhaust system and a unique side stripe treatment.

Mirroring the 'Cuda was Dodge's Challenger R/T and the Challenger T/A. The Challenger, though, was built on a longer, 112-inch wheelbase.

The mighty 1970 Boss 429 engine.

1970 Cougar Eliminator.

All 1970 Boss 429s came with a black hood scoop.

1970 Hemi 'Cuda convertible—one of only 9 made.

1971

For 1971, the Mustang got a new body and a new big-block engine, the 429CJ with 370 or 375 hp. The Mach 1 remained as the Mustang performance model, but the base engine was now a regular 302-cubic-inch V8. Optional engines, besides the 429, were several versions of the 351 Cleveland. The Boss 429 was no longer available.

Wild colors were common, as exemplified by this Panther Pink 1970 'Cuda.

The last Boss Mustang—the 1971 Boss 351.

Designed to compete with the Boss 302 and Z/28, the 1970 AAR 'Cuda was powered by a 340 6-bbl. engine.

1970 Plum Crazy Plymouth Challenger.

Replacing the Boss 302 was the Boss 351. It followed the theme established by the Boss 302, with the exception that the 302 engine was replaced by a high-performance version of the 351 rated at 330 hp. Only 1,806 were built.

Camaro styling differed only in details, but it was obvious that the Super Sport Camaro's days were numbered. The optional 396 V8 was rated at only 300 hp, while the Z/28 got by with a 330-hp, 350-cubic-inch small-block. In fact, the 396 was finally dropped after the 1972 model year.

Bucking the trend was the Firebird. Two new engines were made available: a 325-hp 455 V8, standard on the Formula 455 and the Trans Am, and a 335-hp 455 HO optional.

The Cougar Eliminator was gone, but the 429 was optionally available. The Cougar by this time, was gaining weight and getting away from a performance image, focusing instead on luxury in the coming years.

The Javelin was restyled for the last time, while the AMX became a separate Javelin model, no longer a two-seater. Besides styling changes, the 390 engine was enlarged to 401 cubic inches.

1971 'Cuda got the infamous "Cheese grater" grille.

1971 'Cuda got an even more prominent side treatment.

For 1971, the Challenger featured only minimal styling changes.

AMC's AMX pocket-sized musclecar—1970 was the last year it was produced as a 2-seater.

1971 AMC Javelin/AMX.

The Plymouth 'Cuda and Dodge Challenger got a mild facelift with the same basic engines carried over from 1970. The AAR 'Cuda and Challenger T/A were dropped, however.

Although the Camaro could still be had with a 396 big-block in 1972 and the Firebird would soldier on with various editions of the 455 V8 until 1976, '71 was the end of the Pony musclecars. The 351CJ Mustangs of 1972-73 could not equal the performance of the old big-blocks, the Boss 351 was history, and all big-block engines were dropped from the 'Cuda and Challenger option lists. The 'Cuda and Challenger would last only until 1974. The Javelin, too, was dropped after the 1974 model year.

1971 Cougar.

COMPACT MUSCLE

If big engines and catchy names sold cars, as Detroit thinking went, why not apply the same formula to compact cars?

The typical compacts of the 1960s were the smallest cars that Detroit manufacturers produced, but they were still considerably bigger than European small cars, and compared with cars of

A bit on the plain side, the 1969 Chevy Nova SS396 was a potent performer.

A pair of Dodge
Dart GTSs—both
powered by the
275-hp 340-cubic-
inch small-block.

today, some would be considered full-size cars! The typical Detroit compact was pretty spartan—just the basics: usually a six-cylinder engine with column-mounted manual shifter and perhaps an optional radio. Certainly, these cars could be optioned up, usually with smallish V8 engines and automatic transmissions, but even so, there really wasn't such a thing as a "luxury" compact as there are today. Detroit built them as afterthoughts, to satisfy the market segment that wanted them, as the big money was made on the full-size and intermediate models.

It was during the early Sixties that the compact gained its popularity. Suddenly, everyone wanted one. Less expensive to run and maintain, compacts were a more affordable entry-level car. The compact leader in the late Fifties/early Sixties was the Rambler American. Soon it was joined by the Chevrolet Chevy II/Nova, Ford's Falcon, the Plymouth Valiant and the Dodge Lancer.

Probably the best-known compact that became a full-fledged musclecar was Chevrolet's Nova. Introduced in 1962, the Nova was available with a Super Sport option in 1963 and a small 283-cubic-inch V8 in 1964. Engine sizes kept getting larger as the Sixties progressed, with a 350-hp 327-cubic-inch small-block becoming optional in 1966. Complementing a major restyle in 1968 was the availability of the Chevrolet big-block V8, displac-

Overkill is an apt description for the 1969 Dart GTS powered by the 440 big-block.

Even AMC produced a compact musclecar—the SC/Hurst Rambler.

ing 396 cubic inches with power ratings of 325 or 375 hp. Only 901 were sold, but still it meant that other manufacturers would soon be offering bigger engines too on their compacts.

It was obvious that the 396 was popular on the Nova as 7,209 cars got this engine in 1968 but only 5,567 in 1970. It was dropped in 1971 with a 350-cubic-inch small-block taking up the performance chores.

In the overall scheme of things, the big-block Novas represented a small fraction of the line's total production; the typical Nova buyer was interested in economy.

Ford never went the big-block route with the Falcon. Following its initial success, Ford promoted the Mustang (on which it was based) as a car for everyone and, as such,

The 1971 Plymouth Duster 340.

a properly optioned Mustang had the makings of an economy compact.

Of the Chrysler compacts, the Dodge Dart got a good jolt in the engine compartment in 1968 when the new 340-cubic-inch small-block V8 was introduced in the Dart GTS model. It was also available in 1969.

There was also a small run of 440-cubic-inch-equipped Dart GTS's in 1969. Although powerful, these were ill-handling cars and lacked power steering, power brakes and air conditioning.

Far more popular was the Plymouth Duster, which was introduced in 1970. With the optional 340 engine, the Duster 340 was exceptionally fast because of its light weight. A companion model, the 1971-72 Dodge Demon, shared the same basic body platform and 340 engine. The 340 engine was replaced by a 360 in 1974, but by then, the Duster had lost most of its oomph. Dodge also dropped the name Demon in 1973, renaming the car the Dart Sport. As with other Chrysler engines, the 1970-71 340s produce the most power, 275 hp.

The 1971 AMC Hornet SC/360.

Even American Motors took a stab at producing a compact musclecar. This was the 1969 Hurst SC/Rambler powered by AMCs biggest engine, the 390. Only 1,512 were produced. AMC tried once again with the 1971 Hornet SC/360, powered by AMC's 360 engine, but only 784 were produced.

The compact musclecars never caught on in the same way as the intermediates and pony-based cars. In some cases, they may have been as fast as the bigger cars, but their plain styling and conservative image just didn't appeal to the typical enthusiast.

The Demon 340 was Dodge's version of the Plymouth Duster.

1965 Buick Riviera.

FULL-SIZE MUSCLE

Prior to the Pontiac GTO, most of the high-performance American cars were full-size cars. The big cars had bigger engines, and usually better performance. Chrysler introduced the 300 Letter series in 1955 with the C300 and these big cars were powered by the most powerful Chrysler engines at the time. Even though they were fast and race versions won many races, they were not too popular on the street because they were very expensive.

Dodge and Plymouth's performance models, such as the Dodge D-500 and the Plymouth Fury, were big cars. A full-size Plymouth that was introduced in the musclecar era was the Fury S/23 and Fury GT of 1970-71. Most were powered by the 440-cubic-inch big-block, but the Fury S/23 could be had with smaller engines as well. They were interesting cars, but they didn't sell well.

There was also a limited run of 500 1970 Chrysler 300Hs modified by Hurst, which, with the Fury, was the extent of Chrysler Corp.'s involvement with full-size performance cars in the early 1970s.

1965 Pontiac Catalina 2+2.

In 1961, Chevrolet introduced the Impala SS and special versions of the 409-cubic-inch big-block engine. These cars earned a reputation for high performance. The 409 was dropped during the 1965 model year and replaced by the Mark IV series big-blocks, the 396 in 1965 and the 427 in 1966. Of course, it was the Impala SS that got most of the attention, but lesser full-size Chevrolets, such as the Biscayne, could be optioned with the 427 engine. The year 1969 was the last for the Impala SS and the availability of high-performance engines in Chevrolet's full-size

**1966 Ford
Galaxie 500
7-litre.**

1967 Buick Wildcat.

427-powered 1968 Chevrolet Biscayne.

line. A performance image no longer sold big cars.

The big Fords were the Galaxy 500XLs and the best of these were powered by 427-cubic-inch engines with dual four-barrel carburetors. The Galaxy was restyled in 1965 and even though the 427 engine and later in 1966, the 428, were available, the big

**1970 Plymouth
Sport Fury S/23.**

Fords had lost most of their performance image to the Mustang. Like the big Chevrolets, it was luxury that interested the big-car buyer.

Pontiac didn't give up full-size cars completely when the GTO came out; buyers so inclined could get high-horsepower engines in the full-size cars such as the Bonneville and 2+2. These cars, however, did not enjoy the same reputation as in the early 1960s.

Even Buick produced high-powered Wildcats and Rivieras, but because of their high cost, their popularity was very limited.

While these big cars had the same basic performance engines as the intermediates, they weren't as fast simply because of their size. As the Sixties progressed, all Detroit cars got larger and heavier, thereby negating some of their performance potential. But, as such, they are an interesting by-product of the musclecar era.

MUSCLECAR GREATS
PHOTO CREDITS

Special thanks to MuscleCars Magazine for providing the photographs used in this book.

Pages 4-5, Dave Lundy; Pages 8-9, 1965 Olds 4-4-2, Paul McLaughlin; Page 10, Dave Lundy; Page 11, Peter Sessler; Page 14, Dave Lundy; Page 19, 1969 Road Runner, Jeff Bauer; 1968 GTX, Peter Sessler; Pages 20-21, Peter Sessler; Page 22, 1969 Chevelle, Dave Lundy; Pages 22-23, Peter Sessler; Pages 28-29, Peter Sessler; Pages 30-31, 1970 Chevelle, Peter Sessler; Page 31, 1970 Olds 4-4-2, Sue Elliott; Pages 32-33, Peter Sessler; Pages 38-39, Peter Sessler; Page 40, 1970 Road Runner, Peter Sessler; Pages 44-45, Peter Sessler; Page 46, Mike Henninger; Page 48, Bart R. Orlans; Page 50, Dave Lundy; Pages 52-53, Peter Sessler; Page 54, Peter Sessler; Page 55 (bottom), Peter Sessler; Page 56, Boss 429, Peter Sessler; Boss 302, Paul McLaughlin; Page 58, Peter Sessler; Page 61, 1969 Camaro, Peter Sessler; Page 62, Z/28, Peter Sessler; Page 63, Peter Sessler; Page 64, Peter Sessler; Page 66, 1970 Cougar, Jim Maxwell; Page 68, 1970 AAR Cuda, Peter Sessler; Page 71,1970 AMX, Nick Wright; Page 74 (bottom), Peter Sessler; Pages 76-77, Peter Sessler; Page 80, Peter Sessler; Pages 82-83, Dave Lundy; Page 84, Linda Boulis; Page 86, Dave Lundy; Pages 92-93, Jim Campisano; Pages 94-95, Peter Sessler. All other photos, MuscleCars Magazine archives.

On the cover—Mark J. O'Malia's 1968 Dodge Charger R/T powered by the 426 Hemi engine—one of 475 made.
Photo: Peter Sessler